Nonno is my Grandfather

written by
Bruna DiGiuseppe-Bertoni

illustrated by
Aurora Pagano

About the Author

Bruna Di Giuseppe-Bertoni was born in Rome Italy.
As an artist, her passion is painting and writing.
She has won literary awards for her poetry in Canada
and Italy. She has been published in Italian and English.
Her books for children: "I call my grandmother Nonna"
& "A day in the life of the Befana" as well as her father's
diary of his life. Her work is dedicated to her family,
six grandchildren, and three great-grandchildren.

"Nonno is my Grandfather"
is dedicated to my 6 grand-children
and 3 great-grand-children.

My nonno Emilio walked me to my first day of school.
I was in kindergarten and the teacher was at the door greeting us.

I didn't understand much of what was said.
My Nonno and Nonna spoke to me in Italian.

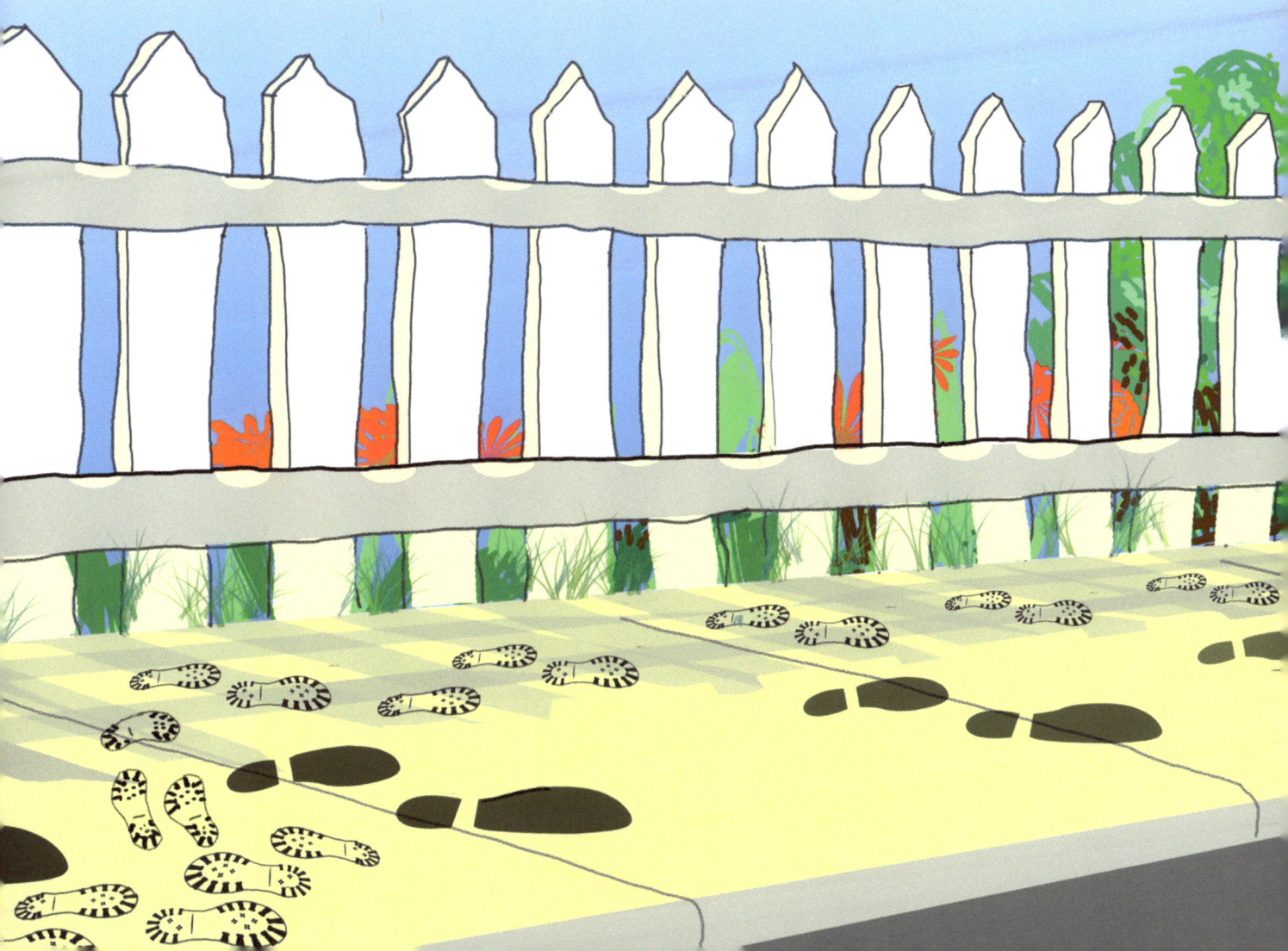

"Good morning." said the teacher.
"Buon Giorno. (Good Morning)" said my Nonno.

"And who is with you, your grandfather?" smiled the teacher. "No!, He is my Nonno." I turned around and waved to him and he said "Ciao. (Goodbye)".

During recess Miss Rosa asked me, "You call your grandfather Nonno Emilio? Why do you have the same name as you grandfather?"
I did not know what to answer.
How confusing, Emilio was puzzled!

He waited for his grandfather to pick him up at school and asked him about their names.
"Yes, it's confusing!" said Nonno, "It's an old tradition", he explained.
Soon, Emilio discovered some of his friends, being from different cultures have the same custom.

My classmate Pasquale is Italian too, we say, "Ciao" we both like pizza.
(A noi piace mangiare la pizza.)
He has the same name as his nonno! "Pasquale" but we call him "Pat".

My friend Pedro comes from Mexico, his grandfather is Hugo Pedro Sr., he runs a farm and he calls him 'Abuelo'. Pedro's father's name is Hugo Pedro Jr.
They bring Vegetables and fruit from the Food Terminal to stores.
It's been three generations.
(Pedro viene dal Messico, il suo nonno si chiamava Hugo Pedro)

Harold Quon is from China, his grandfather has a restaurant and they cook Chinese Food. He calls his grandfather Yeh Yeh, his name is Harold Sr. (Jonathan è Cinese, il suo nonno ha un ristorante e cucina il cibo cinese). He has a great-grandmother and they call her Zeng Zù Mù.

Fred's grandfather came from England by ship, he was in the war. (Lui era in Guerra ed è venuto in Canada con la nave, come mio nonno). Fred said that his grandmother came later to join him. He calls his grandparents "Grandpa and Granma". He is a butcher.

Emilio loves his grandfather and after school or Sunday's gathering he likes to be with him. They always have something fun to do together.
(Io e nonno abbiamo sempre molto da fare).
It depends on the time of year what we do, for it is always different.
He knows how to fix anything that is broken in the house.
(Lui sa come riparare quello che si rompe in casa)

He will fix a water leak; change the electrical wire to accommodate Nonna. He has remodeled his home many times, and did it on his own. ("Nonno è un tutto fare")

After the Christmas holidays, nonno starts to prepare to make prosciutto and sausages.
(Dopo il Natale, nonno si prepara per curare e confezionare il prosciutto, e salcicce.)

When the weather starts to get warm he prepares to plant seeds in his green house. Later when it is time to plant, he will put the tiny plants in the Vegetable garden.
(Quando è il tempo di piantare, metterà le piantine nel'orto.)
Nonna will only attend to her flower garden.
(Nonna si occupa solo del giardino di fiori.)

The BIG family reunion often comes around "Tomatoes sauce time!"
(La grande riunione della famiglia è nel tempo della salsa di pomodori). It will start early September.

A week is spent on preparation and two or three days to complete the home made salsa sauce "Salsa fatta in casa".

One day we went to see zio Augusto. My grandfather calls him 'Chief'. because he is the older brother and 'head of the family'. It is September and it is time for making wine. Zio Augusto chooses the right grapes and taught my nonno Emilio how to make the best wine. It takes weeks to prepare. When it was ready, Nonno and Zio get together and taste the wine in the Cantina.. (cellar). They played the game of 'one glass for me and one for you!'
('un bicchiere a me e uno a te!) Getting together was also to have fun and party! Zio Augusto entertained us with his accordian, playing songs as old as my great-grandfather. We danced all night to songs like La Romanina, Oi Mari', and 'O Sole Mio'. When Nonno was ready to go, he said "Bye Chief, see you on Monday."

My nonno speaks to me in Italian. (Parliamo solo in Italiano.) English was very hard to learn when he worked only with Italians. (Lavorava solo con amici Italiani.) Most were "Paesani" and they only spoke the dialect from where they came from. (Parlavano un dialetto diverso dal'uno con l'altro.) That alone was a challenge. (Era una grande sfida) At home only Italian was spoken. (In casa si parlava solo in Italiano.)

Sunday lunch at Nonno's house was a treat. (Pranzo a casa di nonno era un divertimento) As soon as lunch was over we played cards; seriously! (Finito il pranzo si giocava a carte. Seriamente!)

Briscola is the game often played with Italian cards with suits of swords, clubs, cups, and coins. (Briscola è spesso giocata con le carte italiane vestite di spade, bastoni, coppe e denari.)
"Nonno it's your turn to deal the cards." I tell him. (Nonno sei tu che devi dare le carte). "Ok!" He shuffles the cards and deals three cards each. ("Bene!" Mischia le carte e da tre carte per uno).

Two to six people can play. We are 2 players.
(Si puó giocare con due a sei persone. Siamo in due a giocare)
The 7th card determines the trump suit that will rule the briscola.
(La settima carta determina la briscola.)
It was fun when Nonno didn't win and he would be upset!!!!
He was funny and we laughed!
(Il divertimento era quando Nonno non vinceva e si aggitava.
Parlava un'altra lingua "@$%^…..%#@….")

My Nonno was born in a very small village in Italy, in the region of Abruzzo, province of Aquila. (Nonno nacque in un piccolo paese in Italia nella regione dell'Abruzzo, provincia Acquila) (Lui raccontava storielle.)
He did not know how to read or write. Where he lived there was no school. His father, who was my great-grandfather died working as a woodcutter. His name was Giovanni.

Nonno had 3 brothers and a sister. (Da piccolo viveva su una montagna in un paesino chiamato Tufo Alto. Il mio bis-nonno lavorando nel bosco come falegname. Si chiamava Giovanni. Aveva tre fratelli e una sorella)
In 1939 at the age of 19 he was called to serve in the military.
(Nel 1939 a l'età di 19 anni, fù chiamato per fare il soldato)
Seven months later Italy was at war. He was shipped to North Africa and did not return until 1946. He was a prisoner of war in England for 6 years. (Sette mesi dopo in l'Italia ci fù la querra. Fù mandato nel Nord Africa e non ritornò fino al 1946. Fù prigioniero in Inghilterra per 6 anni.)

He met Nonna in Rome just after the war ended, and were married in 1951. 14 years later they came to Canada with 3 children.
(Lui incontrò nonna a Roma subito dopo la Guerra, e si sposarono nel 1951. Quattordici anni dopo emigrarono in Canada con 3 bambini).

When Nonno left Italy to come to Toronto, he was working in construction, bulding scaffolding for tall buildings. (Nonno lavorava per una costruzione dove si usava struttura di ponti per palazzi alti.)

Scaffolding is a temporary bridge, used to support the men while they are building the walls. His work was very important. (Il suo lavoro era molto importante.) He had to be precise and fearless. (Doveva essere preciso e senza paura.) One day he received a phone call asking him if he would work on a very important project. It was to build the scaffold to work on the CN Tower project.

He tells us stories on how it was build.
(Nonno racconta come la Torre fù costruita.)
To build the Tower they worked around the clock, 24 hours 5 days a week.
(Si lavorava 24 ore al giorno)
It's as high as 147 buildings; it took 40,500 cubic meters of concrete (cement) and lots of steel to build it.

It was completed March 1975, when "Olga" the giant helicopter lifted a big antenna and placed it on top of the tower, my dad and everyone was watching it on T.V.
Nonno was crying happy tears. (Nonno piangeva per la contentezza)
He said, proudly, "Italians build Toronto".
(Disse: 'Noi Italiani abbiamo costruito Toronto)

When Nonno and I have a few hours left to spare he takes me to the Italian bar "Abbruzzo social club" for a gelato and he has an espresso.
His old friend Stefano says: "Emilio, let's play scopa like the old days".
("Emilio, giochiamo a scopa come i tempi passati! Ti ricordi?")
"Next time Stefano..Alla prossima!" "We must hurry Emilio, nonna is waiting." (Nonna aspetta)

Nonno was born in Abruzzo and although he lived his entire life in Rome, he was still attached to his paese. However, the Roman influenced him and he only spoke the Roman dialect and he loved the Roma soccer team. The team's colors are red and yellow…'Romanista'.
He was proud of his heritage and of his birth place.

www.ingramcontent.com/pod-product-compliance
Lightning Source LLC
Chambersburg PA
CBHW041436010526
44118CB00002B/92